DATE DUE		
MAR 1 0 0		
JUL 03 02		

6/00

JACKSON COUNTY
Library Services

HEADQUARTERS
413 West Main Street
Medford, Oregon 97501

Festivals *of the* World

ETHIOPIA

Gareth Stevens Publishing

Written by
ELIZABETH BERG

Edited by
KEN CHANG

Designed by
LYNN CHIN

Picture research by
SUSAN JANE MANUEL

First published in North America in 1999 by
Gareth Stevens Publishing
1555 North RiverCenter Drive, Suite 201
Milwaukee, Wisconsin 53212 USA

For a free color catalog describing Gareth
Stevens' list of high-quality books and multimedia
programs, call
1-800-542-2595 (USA)
or 1-800-461-9120 (Canada).
Gareth Stevens Publishing's Fax: (414) 225-0377.

© TIMES EDITIONS PTE LTD 1999
Originated and designed by
Times Books International
an imprint of Times Editions Pte Ltd
Times Centre, 1 New Industrial Road
Singapore 536196
Printed in Malaysia

Library of Congress Cataloging-in-Publication Data:
Berg, Elizabeth, 1953–
Ethiopia / by Elizabeth Berg.
p. cm. — (Festivals of the world)
Includes bibliographical references and index.
Summary: Describes how the culture of Ethiopia is
reflected in its many festivals, including Ganna,
Maskal, and the Victory of Adwa Day.
ISBN 0-8368-2032-0 (lib. bdg.)
1. Festivals—Ethiopia—Juvenile literature.
2. Ethiopia—Social life and customs—Juvenile
literature. [1. Festivals—Ethiopia. 2. Holidays—
Ethiopia. 3. Ethiopia—Social life and customs.]
I. Title. II. Series.
GT4889.E8B47 1999
394.26963—dc21 99-10728

1 2 3 4 5 6 7 8 9 03 02 01 00 99

CONTENTS

It's Festival Time . . .

The **Amharic** word for festival is *kibre beal* [kib-ree BAHL]. Ethiopians work hard, so when festival time comes around, they make sure they enjoy it. Every one of their 13 months has at least one festival in it, and a festival means feasting, dancing, parading, and having fun. Every religion also has a holiday to celebrate. So come along and join the fun! It's festival time in Ethiopia . . .

WHERE'S ETHIOPIA?

Ethiopia is located in eastern Africa. It is a landlocked country bordered by Kenya, Somalia, Djibouti, Eritrea, and Sudan. Ethiopia is often called the Roof of Africa because most of the country lies on a very high plateau.

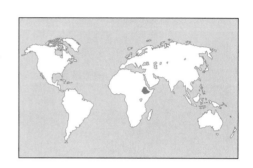

Who are the Ethiopians?

Ethiopia is home for many nationalities, and Ethiopians are famous for their **patriotic** spirit. The Amhara, Tigray, Oromo, Somali, and Gurage are the major Ethiopian ethnic groups. More than 80 languages are spoken in Ethiopia!

The history of the Ethiopian people is ancient. Their early ancestors, the Aksumites, were trading with distant parts of the world hundreds of years before the birth of Christ.

Christianity and Islam are the main religions in Ethiopia, but other religions, such as **animism** and Judaism, are practiced by small groups of the population.

The Oromo people of Ethiopia wear necklaces as lucky charms. You can learn how to make one on page 28.

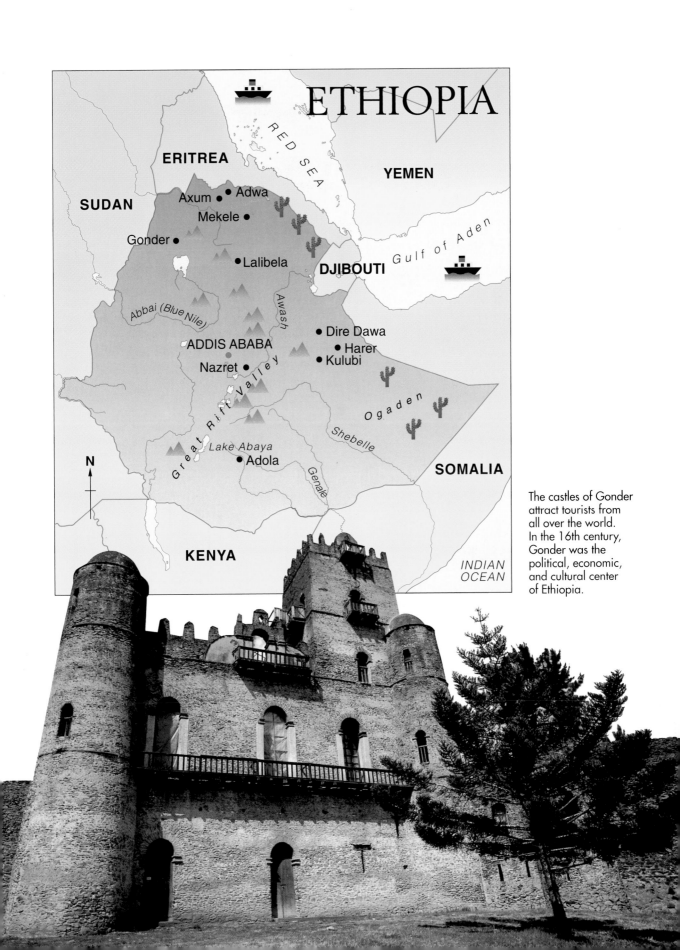

ETHIOPIA

RED SEA

ERITREA

SUDAN

YEMEN

Axum ● ● Adwa

Mekele ●

Gonder ●

Gulf of Aden

Lalibela ●

DJIBOUTI

Abbai (Blue Nile)

Awash

ADDIS ABABA

Dire Dawa ●

● Harer

Nazret ● ● Kulubi

Great Rift Valley

Ogaden

Shebelle

Lake Abaya

● Adola

Genale

SOMALIA

N

KENYA

INDIAN OCEAN

The castles of Gonder
attract tourists from
all over the world.
In the 16th century,
Gonder was the
political, economic,
and cultural center
of Ethiopia.

WHEN'S THE KIBRE BEAL?

Most Ethiopians follow the **Julian calendar**, which has 12 months of 30 days, plus a 13th month of either five or six days. Because Ethiopian Muslims use a **lunar** calendar, which follows the changing phases of the moon, the dates of Muslim holidays change every year.

Ethiopia has only three seasons during the year: *bega* (the dry, spring season, from September through February), *belg* (the short rainy season from March through April), and *kiremt* (the long rainy season from May through August).

How about some sweets? We love to celebrate with good food!

BEGA
- ✪ **ENKUTATASH**
- ✪ **MASKAL**
- ✪ **KULUBI (FEAST OF SAINT GABRIEL)**—Ethiopians honor their favorite angel, Saint Gabriel, every year on December 28th. People go on a **pilgrimage** to Saint Gabriel's church in Kulubi, a small town near Dire Dawa. Many bring their babies to be baptized.
- ✪ **GANNA**
- ✪ **TIMKAT**

BELG
- ✪ **VICTORY OF ADWA DAY**
- ✪ **GOOD FRIDAY AND EASTER**—
  These important religious holidays are
  celebrated by Ethiopia's **Coptic Christians**.

KIREMT
- ✪ **VICTORY DAY**—This holiday is the
  anniversary of Italy's defeat in Africa
  during World War II.
- ✪ **NATIONAL DAY**—On May 28th, street
  parades commemorate the founding of the
  Federal Democratic Republic of Ethiopia.
- ✪ **BUHE**

MUSLIM HOLIDAYS
- ✪ **MAWLID (BIRTHDAY OF THE PROPHET)**
- ✪ **RAMADAN**—For 30 days, Muslims fast from
  sunrise to sunset. In the evening, they feast
  and celebrate.
- ✪ **EID EL-FITR**—This holiday marks
  the end of Ramadan. Muslims pray
  in the **mosque**, visit family and
  friends, and have a big feast.
- ✪ **EID EL-ADHA**—Muslims slaughter
  sheep in honor of Ibrahim's
  willingness to sacrifice his son.

Come celebrate Timkat with us! Let's dance and have a feast!

7

CELEBRATING SPRINGTIME

I t's early September—the end of the rainy season in the Ethiopian highlands. The weather is sunny and pleasant, and the yellow maskal daisies are in bloom. What a perfect time to celebrate the New Year! Enkutatash (en-koo-TAH-tash), the Ethiopian New Year, falls on September 11th. *Enkutatash* means "gift of jewels." The name comes from the story of the Queen of Sheba. After the queen returned to Ethiopia from Jerusalem, King Solomon sent her a gift of jewelry. On the eve of Enkutatash, people light fires in their homes to welcome the new year.

This man is celebrating spring by beating out the rhythm of a happy song on his drum.

These Ethiopian boys are enjoying spring's first flowers.

Enjoying nature

Enkutatash is also the time to celebrate the beginning of fine weather and new life. Ethiopians cover their floors with freshly cut grass. Children dressed all in white go from door to door singing and offering bouquets of wildflowers to every lady of the house. In return, the children might receive a little bread or money or some small gifts.

Maskal

A few weeks after Enkutatash, Ethiopians again celebrate springtime with the festival of Maskal (mehs-KEHL), the Finding of the True Cross. Legend has it that Queen Helena of Rome had people set fire to long poles, and the smoke from the fires pointed to the spot where Christ's cross was buried. A piece of the actual cross was given to Ethiopia's kings to thank them for protecting Egyptian Christians living in Ethiopia.

Time for a party

Ethiopians celebrate Maskal with a lot of dancing and feasting. The warm spring weather, the blooming flowers, and the excitement of a new year make a wonderful atmosphere for a party. Ethiopians are too lively to just sit around at home—the proper place for a Maskal party is always outside in the sun!

Above: Maskal is a time for Ethiopians to get together for some singing and dancing.

The Maskal parade

The best place to celebrate Maskal is in Addis Ababa. Every year, the city has a big parade, with dancers, musicians, colorful floats, and marching soldiers. Schoolchildren sing and dance to the drum rhythms. Everyone in Addis Ababa turns out to watch the Maskal parade.

This Ethiopian priest is waving a flag in the famous Maskal parade of Addis Ababa.

A bonfire is the main event of the Maskal celebration.

Light the bonfire

At sunset, it's time to light the bonfire. On Maskal eve, men set up a large pole, called a *demera* (dem-eh-RAH), in an open space. The next day, women and girls decorate smaller eucalyptus poles with yellow maskal flowers. These poles are set up around the demera. As the sun goes down, the poles are lit to make a bonfire. People dance around the bonfire singing Maskal songs and feeding the flames with torches. It's good fun, but the fire is also considered a sacred fire. The next morning, people stick their fingers in the ashes and draw the sign of the cross on their foreheads.

Think about this

The Queen of Sheba is very important to Ethiopians because a long line of kings descended from her. These kings ruled Ethiopia for 3,000 years, which is the longest monarchy in the world! How old is your country?

11

GANNA

January 7th in Ethiopia is Christmas! Ethiopians call it Ganna (gehn-NAH). Most Ethiopian Christians belong to their own special church, the Ethiopian Orthodox Church, which has over 20 million worshippers. The traditions of the Ethiopian Orthodox Church are very different from the traditions of Christian churches in America. For example, Ethiopians believe that Christ was born on January 7th instead of December 25th. Also, their churches look more like Jewish synagogues than steepled, Christian churches.

The Ethiopian Orthodox Church was founded in the fourth century, which makes it one of the oldest Christian churches in the world. A famous and exciting story tells how Christianity came to Ethiopia.

This boy is holding a cross for the Ganna church service. Ethiopia is famous for its beautifully decorated crosses.

The story of Frumentius and Aedesius

A long time ago, two young Syrian brothers, named Frumentius and Aedesius, were traveling by ship along the coast of the Red Sea. Suddenly, they were caught in a violent storm. The ship overturned, but the two boys were rescued by Ethiopian fishermen. King Ezana of Axum (a kingdom in northern Ethiopia) took the brothers into his household and raised them as his sons. As the boys grew up, King Ezana came to respect their wisdom, especially that of the younger brother, Aedesius. The King later made Aedesius his adviser.

Both Frumentius and Aedesius were Christians, and they soon convinced King Ezana to convert to Christianity. King Ezana first agreed to let Frumentius and Aedesius preach in his kingdom; then he made Christianity the official religion of Axum.

The Ganna eve church service in Lalibela takes place by candlelight. Pilgrims from all over Ethiopia come to Lalibela to celebrate Ganna.

13

A day to relax

Ethiopians work hard all year long just so they'll have enough to eat. Days of feasting, such as Ganna, are the rare times when they can relax and have fun. Ethiopians have a saying: If you don't laugh on Ganna, you won't laugh all year long!

The exciting game of ganna is played only on Christmas. Ganna is a rough game, but it's a lot of fun!

Traditions and rituals

For several days before Ganna, Ethiopians fast during the morning. They don't eat before noon, and they avoid eating any meat, eggs, cheese, butter, or milk. On the eve of Ganna, church services last until after midnight. When the services are over, people begin the Ganna celebrations by breaking their fast with a big feast. The following day, Ethiopians feast and play games with their families and friends. One popular **pastime** is a game called *ganna*.

Markets sell religious paintings during Ganna.

Let's play ganna

During the afternoon on Ganna, men and older boys get together to play the ancient, traditional game of ganna. Ethiopians believe shepherds played this game in the fields when they first heard about the birth of Christ. Ganna is a rough game, similar to field hockey, and players sometimes get hurt. In the evening, after the game is over, people exchange gifts and eat and drink some more.

One man, named Abebe Bikila, went from being a good ganna player to being one of the greatest athletes ever. As a boy, he liked to play ganna. He later became a marathon runner and won gold medals at the Olympic Games in 1960 and 1964.

Think about this
Ganna is a Christmas pastime for Ethiopians. What pastimes do Americans enjoy at Christmas? Sometimes it's more fun to watch a rough game like ganna than to play it. What particularly rough sport do many Americans prefer to watch instead of play?

These people are preparing the Ganna feast. Both children and adults help with the cooking.

TIMKAT

A great drum beats out the message—it's time for the procession. The chief priest appears in the doorway of the church, dressed in shimmering robes. Another priest comes behind him, carrying, on his head, the *tabot* (TAH-boht), which is a small box covered with a cloth. A line of priests follows, each one carrying a brightly colored umbrella and an **ornate** gold or silver cross. Altar boys wearing shiny crowns are next in line, followed by a band of folk musicians. The townspeople join them as they walk. From time to time, the procession pauses to chant and dance. It is the eve of Timkat (TIM-keht), and every town in Ethiopia is escorting its tabot out of its home in the church.

A priest carefully carries a tabot over his head during the Timkat procession.

What is a tabot?

Every Ethiopian church keeps a tabot. The tabot is an imitation of the wooden Ark of the Covenant—the box containing the Ten Commandments God gave to Moses. Ethiopians believe that the true Ark of the Covenant is kept at St. Mary of Zion Church in Axum, and they have a story about how it got there.

Long ago, Ethiopia was ruled by a queen named Makeda, also known as the Queen of Sheba. After hearing about a wise king named Solomon in Jerusalem, the queen left Ethiopia to meet him. Makeda fell in love with King Solomon and married him. Their son, Menelik I, founded Ethiopia's royal dynasty. Once, after visiting his father's court, Menelik took the Ark of the Covenant back with him to Ethiopia. The angry Solomon followed Menelik with his royal army. As the king drew near, Menelik's men were lifted across the Red Sea into Ethiopia. King Solomon then knew that God had meant the Ark to go to Ethiopia.

This painting shows the Queen of Sheba, whose famous story is well known to Jews, Muslims, and Christians. In Ethiopia, she is called Makeda.

17

The tabot's journey

The Timkat procession stops near a pool of water, where the priests of the church guard the tabot through the night. Before daybreak, townspeople gather at the pool. The priest dips a cross and a burning candle into the water, then sprinkles water over the worshippers. Holy men from the church form two long lines and begin an ancient dance. Finally, the procession winds its way back to the church, and it's time for feasting and celebration.

Opposite: This Timkat procession is leaving the church of St. George in Lalibela. The church was carved out of solid rock almost 800 years ago.

A daring game of guks

Just as Ganna is the day to play ganna, Timkat is a time to play **guks** (googs). Guks is a dueling game that originated in ancient Ethiopian warfare. Men pretend to be warriors, wearing lion-mane capes and carrying hippopotamus shields. Mounted on horseback, each warrior rides at full speed down a field, aiming a bamboo lance at his opponent. The good horsemen always put on a thrilling show for the crowd.

Below: There's always lots of action in a Timkat procession. These holy men are dancing and shaking rattles.

CELEBRATING ETHIOPIA

Ethiopia is one of the oldest civilizations in the world. It also has a glorious history of independence. Ethiopia and Liberia are the only two countries in Africa that were never conquered by Europeans.

Ethiopians proudly celebrate their nation's independence. Every year on March 2nd, they celebrate the anniversary of the Victory of Adwa, one of the most important events in African history.

Above: Emperor Menelik II defended Ethiopia from the Italians in 1896.

The decision to fight

On the morning of March 1, 1896, Emperor Menelik II had to make a very difficult decision. The Italian army in Eritrea was advancing south across Ethiopia's northern border. Although Menelik had signed a peace treaty with the Italians in 1889, both sides spent the following years preparing for war. Now it was time for battle, and Ethiopia's precious independence was at stake. At dawn, Menelik launched an attack on the Italian forces in the city of Adwa.

Left: This magnificent statue of Menelik II stands in Addis Ababa, the capital of Ethiopia.

Opposite: This Ethiopian painting depicts the famous Battle of Adwa.

Victory!

Menelik's army of 100,000 Ethiopians surprised and overwhelmed the 20,000 invading Italian troops. By noon, the Battle of Adwa was over. The Italians quickly retreated to Eritrea, and, on the next day, the victory at Adwa was announced to all the Ethiopian people. Ethiopia remained free and independent!

Menelik's victory at the Battle of Adwa was important for several reasons. After defeating Italy in a one-sided battle, Ethiopia gained respect from countries all over the world, especially in Europe and America. Ethiopia emerged as a strong, independent, international power, attracting the attention of **foreign** politicians and businessmen. The brave King Menelik became known not only as a great African leader, but also as a great world leader.

Ethiopia has remained a **beacon** of freedom for all people—Africans, Americans, Europeans, and Asians. They all point to this country's long history of independence as a remarkable achievement.

The royal tomb of King Menelik II in Addis Ababa is the final resting place for one of the greatest rulers in Ethiopian and world history.

A time to celebrate

Ethiopians have celebrated the Victory of Adwa ever since, with big feasts, dancing, and parades. It is a day for Ethiopians to show pride in their country. Ethiopia also has a national day and other holidays to celebrate their country, but Victory of Adwa Day is the most special of all. It helps Ethiopians remember that, no matter how difficult things might be for their country now, they have a lot about which to be proud.

The lively celebrations for Victory of Adwa Day always spill out into the streets.

Think about this

Has your country ever had to defend itself from people who wanted to conquer it? Some of the greatest leaders in the world fought to keep their national independence. What leaders fought for your country's independence?

On Victory of Adwa Day, Ethiopians celebrate who they are and what their country has achieved.

23

MAWLID

I slam reached Ethiopia in the late 7th century, shortly after the religion was founded by Muhammad the Prophet in Arabia. Today, over 10 million Muslims live in Ethiopia, and they celebrate many religious holidays and festivals.

Mawlid [maw-LEED] is an Arabic name for the birthday of Prophet Muhammad. Many Muslims in other countries do not consider Mawlid a major religious festival, but Ethiopian Muslims recognize Mawlid as one of the most sacred days of the year. Mawlid is not a birthday celebration but a time for all Muslims to pray and give thanks to Prophet Muhammad.

These two Ethiopian girls are wearing traditional Muslim clothing.

The tomb of Sheikh Hussein

The Mawlid traditions of Ethiopian Muslims are unique. For many of the Oromo people of Ethiopia, Mawlid is a time to make a holy pilgrimage to the tomb of Sheikh Hussein.

Sheikh Hussein was a holy man who lived hundreds of years ago. The Oromo believe that his tomb has special powers and that just touching it can heal someone who is sick. On Mawlid, thousands of Oromos make the long journey, traveling on foot or on horseback, to Sheikh Hussein's tomb in the highlands. For some, the journey will take as long as six months to complete. During the pilgrimage, the travelers are not allowed to cut their hair or to sleep indoors. When the pilgrims reach the tomb, they smear the dust from its walls on their faces. Outside the tomb, they gather to sing verses in honor of Sheikh Hussein. The Oromos remain at the tomb for a few weeks, trying to absorb its healing power.

This street in Harer has a small market in front of the local mosque. Arabian Muslims founded Harer over a thousand years ago.

THINGS FOR YOU TO DO

On August 19th, Ethiopian children have their own special holiday. It's called Buhe (BOO-hay), and it's a Christian holiday. Buhe celebrates the day Jesus and three of his disciples climbed Mount Tabor (in Israel) to pray. When they reached the top, Jesus' appearance changed—his face and clothing began to glow white. At the bottom of the mountain, some shepherd boys saw the bright light and went up to find out what it was. When the boys didn't come back, their worried families searched for them with torches and bread.

Celebrating Buhe

Buhe is a fun holiday for children—a little like Halloween in America. Children go door-to-door carrying torches and sing at people's houses in hope of receiving bread, money, or a small present.

Giving thanks

When accepting gifts from a household, Ethiopian children make up a blessing to say to the mistress of the house. The fun of celebrating Buhe is not just receiving presents, but also finding creative ways to thank all the generous people.

Compose a blessing

Now it's your turn to make up a blessing. A Buhe blessing is always funny and clever, so get your imagination ready. Your blessing is supposed to bestow good wishes on the household in a humorous way. Here's an example of a Buhe blessing: "May the bedbugs not bite anyone in this good house."

Try to make up several Buhe blessings for your friends and neighbors, then try them out next August 19th!

Things to look for in your library

Day of Delight: A Jewish Sabbath in Ethiopia. J. Brian Pinkney (Dial Books, 1994).
Ethiopia: The Harp of Apollo (Discovery, 1994) (compact disc).
Ethiopia: Land of Plenty. OneWorld magazine's special report on Ethiopia
  (http://www.envirolink.org/oneworld/focus/etiopia/toc.htm).
Ethiopia: The Roof of Africa. Jane Kurtz (Dillon Press, 1991).
A Family from Ethiopia. Julia Waterlow (Raintree/Steck-Vaughn, 1998).
Fire on the Mountain. Jane Kurtz (Simon & Schuster, 1994).
The Lion's Whiskers. Nancy Raines Day (Scholastic, 1995).
Traditional Music of Ethiopia (Playasound, 1994).

MAKE A LUCKY CHARM

E thiopians have some very superstitious traditions that have been passed down for generations. Many of the Oromo people wear charm necklaces for good luck. You can wear one, too. Just follow the steps below, then see if it changes your luck!

You will need:
1. Water
2. Twine
3. Thin stick
4. Paint brushes
5. Modeling clay
6. Paints
7. Paint tray

1 Wet the modeling clay and shape it into oblong pieces of different sizes.

2 While the clay is still wet, lightly poke the surface of the pieces with the stick to make small dots. Near the top of each piece, poke a hole all the way through.

3 When the clay has dried, paint the pieces.

4 Thread the twine through the holes, then knot the twine. Now you have your very own lucky charm!

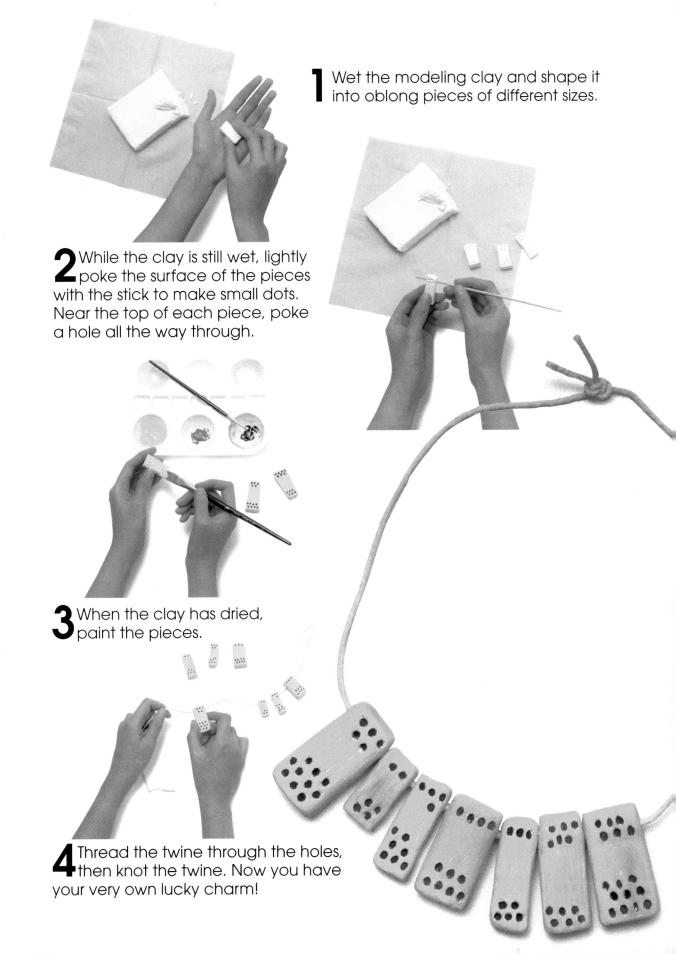

MAKE DABO KOLO

Ethiopians love to feast, and, after a big meal, they love to eat sweets. *Dabo kolo* is a spicy cookie that is a favorite among Ethiopian kids. Cayenne pepper might seem strange in cookies, but you've got to try it!

You will need:

1. Spoon
2. Wooden spoon
3. Measuring spoons
4. 3 tablespoons cayenne pepper
5. ½ teaspoon salt
6. ¼ teaspoon ground cloves
7. 1 teaspoon ground ginger
8. ½ teaspoon ground cinnamon
9. 2 tablespoons light oil
10. 1 cup (140 grams) whole wheat flour
11. 2 teaspoons sugar
12. ⅔ cup (160 milliliters) water
13. Measuring cup
14. Breadboard
15. Small bowl
16. Mixing bowl
17. Baking pan
18. Oven mitt

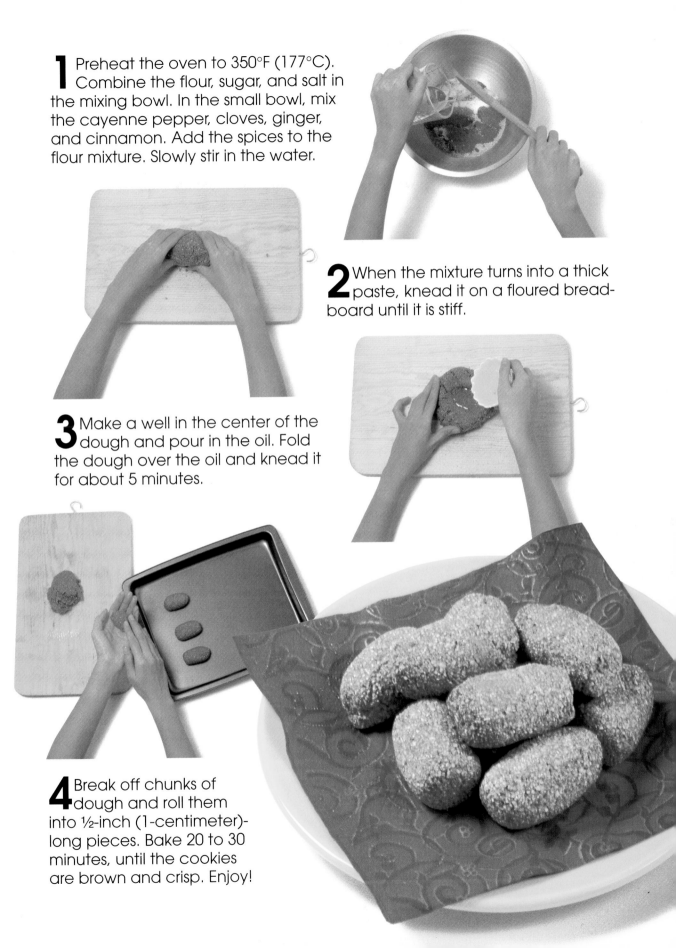

1 Preheat the oven to 350°F (177°C). Combine the flour, sugar, and salt in the mixing bowl. In the small bowl, mix the cayenne pepper, cloves, ginger, and cinnamon. Add the spices to the flour mixture. Slowly stir in the water.

2 When the mixture turns into a thick paste, knead it on a floured bread-board until it is stiff.

3 Make a well in the center of the dough and pour in the oil. Fold the dough over the oil and knead it for about 5 minutes.

4 Break off chunks of dough and roll them into ½-inch (1-centimeter)-long pieces. Bake 20 to 30 minutes, until the cookies are brown and crisp. Enjoy!

GLOSSARY

Amharic, 3	Referring to Amharigna, the national language of Ethiopia.
animism, 4	The belief that all natural things possess souls.
beacon, 22	A signal or guiding light.
Coptic Christians, 7	Followers of the Christian church of Egypt.
foreign, 22	From another country.
ganna, 14	A traditional ball game played by Ethiopians on Christmas.
guks, 19	A game in which horsemen duel with bamboo lances.
Julian calendar, 6	A calendar having 13 months and a total of 365 or 366 days.
lunar, 6	Related to the moon.
mosque, 7	A Muslim place of worship.
ornate, 16	Lavishly decorated.
pastime, 14	An amusing or pleasurable leisure-time activity.
patriotic, 4	Devoted to one's country.
pilgrimage, 6	A journey made for religious reasons.
tabot, 16	A box representing the Ark of the Covenant.

INDEX

Picture credits
Afrika Photo: 12, 13, 14 (bottom), 15;
ANA Press: 24, 25; Camera Press: 28;
Camerapix: 5, 7 (bottom), 10 (bottom),
11, 16, 17, 18, 20 (both), 21, 22;
Embassy of the Federal Democratic
Republic of Ethiopia in Beijing, China:
4, 14 (top), 23 (both); Victor Englebert:
19; David Houser: 3 (top); Bjorn
Klingwall: 8; Christine Osborne: 9; Liba
Taylor: 1, 2, 3 (bottom), 6, 7 (top), 10
(top), 26, 27

Digital scanning by
Superskill Graphics Pte Ltd